Juvenile

W9-CFJ-592

3 1257 01898 7874

GRAPHIC SURVIVAL STORIES

DEFYING DEATH IN THE
WILDERNESS

by Rob Shone

illustrated by James Field

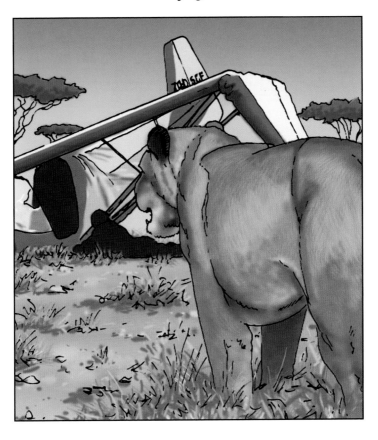

New York

Published in 2010 by The Rosen Publishing Group, Inc.
29 East 21st Street, New York, NY 10010

Designed and produced by
David West Books

Editor: Katharine Pethick

Photo credits:
P4t, Dave Menke/U.S. Fish and Wildlife Service; 4m, Charlie Brenner; 5t, Christophe Meneboeuf; 5b, Clem23; 6m, USDA; 7tb, Sputnikcccp; 7m, Petru Damsa; 44b, Arpingstone; 44m, Retron.

Library of Congress Cataloging-in-Publication Data

Shone, Rob.
 Defying death in the wilderness / Rob Shone ; illustrated by James Field. -- 1st ed.
     p. cm. -- (Graphic survival stories)
 Includes index.
 ISBN 978-1-4358-3531-3 (library binding) -- ISBN 978-1-61532-865-9 (pbk.) -- ISBN 978-1-61532-867-3 (6-pack)
 1. Wilderness survival--Juvenile literature. I. Field, James, 1959- ill. II. Title.
 GV200.5.S56 2010
 613.6'9--dc22

Manufactured in China

CPSIA Compliance Information: Batch #DW0102YA:
For Further Information contact Rosen Publishing, New York, New York at 1-800-237-9932

CONTENTS

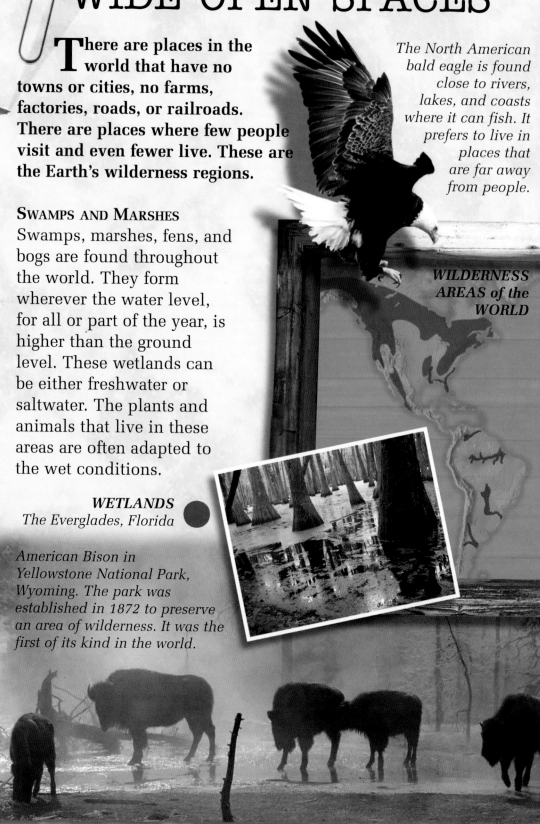

WIDE OPEN SPACES

There are places in the world that have no towns or cities, no farms, factories, roads, or railroads. There are places where few people visit and even fewer live. These are the Earth's wilderness regions.

The North American bald eagle is found close to rivers, lakes, and coasts where it can fish. It prefers to live in places that are far away from people.

SWAMPS AND MARSHES

Swamps, marshes, fens, and bogs are found throughout the world. They form wherever the water level, for all or part of the year, is higher than the ground level. These wetlands can be either freshwater or saltwater. The plants and animals that live in these areas are often adapted to the wet conditions.

WILDERNESS AREAS of the WORLD

WETLANDS
The Everglades, Florida

American Bison in Yellowstone National Park, Wyoming. The park was established in 1872 to preserve an area of wilderness. It was the first of its kind in the world.

FORESTS
Baikal Forest, Russia

FORESTS AND WOODS
The taiga, or boreal forest, is the largest area of forest on the planet. It circles the globe south of the Arctic and is formed largely of coniferous trees. Coniferous forests also grow in more southerly, temperate, and dry regions, as do forests of deciduous trees because they contain a rich mixture of plants and animals.

GRASSLANDS
Mongolian steppe

BUSH AND PLAINS
Bush and scrub are found in areas that are not dry enough to be deserts. Hot summers are followed by warm winters, though in some places the winters can be very cold. The steppes of Asia, prairies of North America and the pampas of Argentina are all grasslands. Here, vast tracts of land are covered by seas of grass. Trees and woody plants get little chance to grow amid the densely packed grass.

SEMIARID BUSH AND SCRUB
Olduvai Gorge, Africa

WILDERNESS SURVIVAL

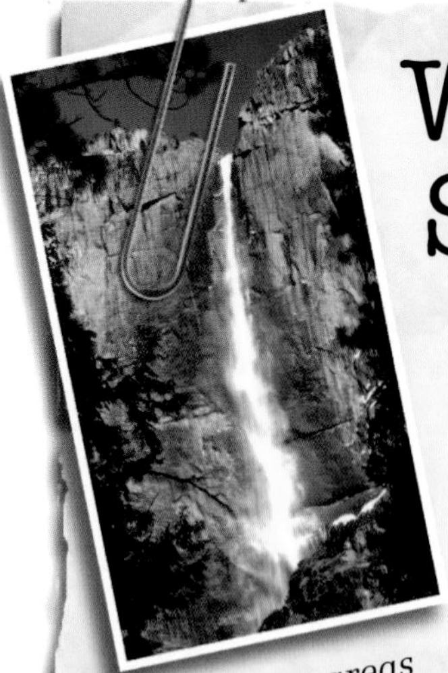

Wilderness areas are often places of outstanding natural beauty.

Getting lost in a town or city can be annoying. But there are street maps to help you find the way, and people to ask for directions. Getting lost in a wilderness is far more serious.

WHERE THE WILD THINGS BITE

The wilderness is home to many creatures. Most are harmless, some are food, a few are deadly. Not all of these savage beasts have large teeth or sharp claws. The hooves and horns of large grazers can cause terrible injuries. However, the world's most dangerous creature is not a lion, a bear, or even a snake, but the tiny mosquito. Malaria, the disease this insect carries, kills millions of people each year.

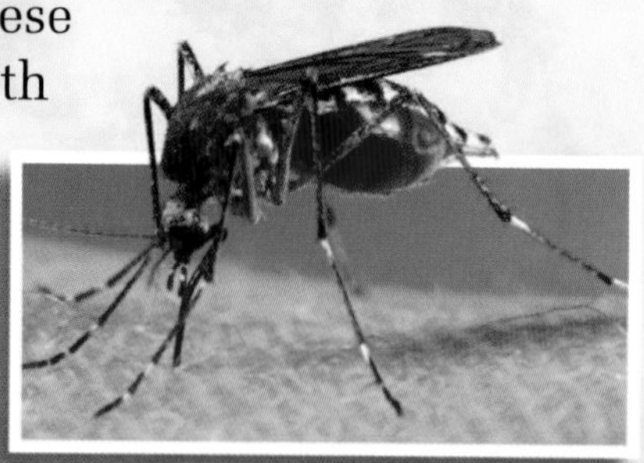

In a wilderness, biting creatures can be very small, like this mosquito (above), or very large, like the grizzly bear (left). Both are dangerous.

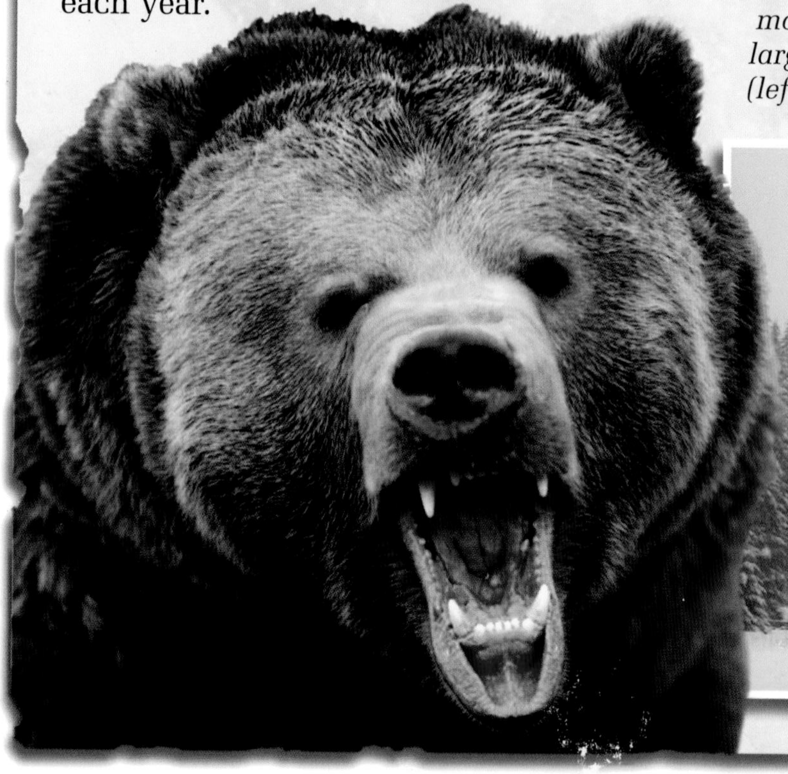

The weather can be as hazardous as any wild animal. A sudden change in conditions can kill.

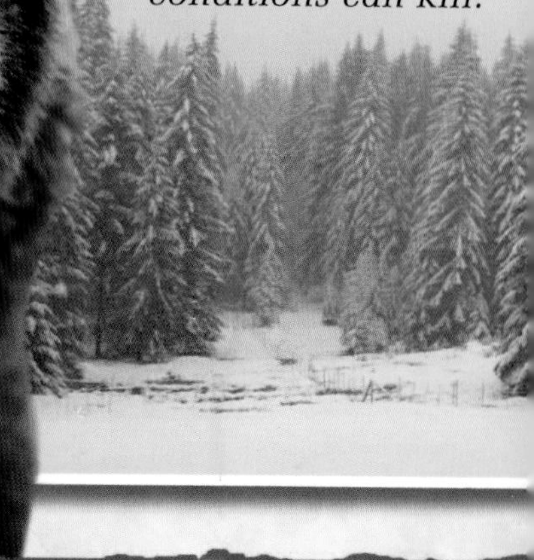

FOOD FOR FREE

It is not impossible to find food in a wilderness. Most animals are edible, as are grass seeds. Fish can be caught with a simple hook and line, and frogs, snakes, lizards, and birds can be eaten. Beware, though—many of these creatures are poisonous, and, in the wild, not all vegetables are good for you. Some plants can kill.

Insects can be a good source of food in a wilderness. Australian witchetty grubs, the larvae of the cossid moth, grow to 4 inches (10 cm) long, and taste like eggs.

Many mushrooms are edible, but a few are lethal. Only an expert can tell the good fungi from the bad.

SURVIVAL TIPS

- **STAY CALM.** A cool head will help you make the right decisions.
- **BUILD A SHELTER.** Protection from the elements is important when trying to survive in a wilderness.
- **BUILD A FIRE.** A fire will keep you warm when it is cold, ward off wild animals, and cook your food.
- **FIND WATER.** Dehydration is a serious threat, even in places that are not dry. Water purification tablets can prevent illness caused by drinking dirty water.
- **FIND FOOD.** The human body can go several weeks without food, but cold weather and increased activity will shorten this period.
- **BE PREPARED.** Wearing the right clothing for the conditions and having the appropriate equipment can save your life.

CAUGHT IN THE CAULDRON OF FIRE
MOUNT ST. HELENS, WASHINGTON, 1980

THE SIX FRIENDS HAD DECIDED ONLY AT THE LAST MINUTE TO GO ON THE CAMPING TRIP. IT WAS MAY 18, 1980, AND THEY HAD CHOSEN THE GREEN RIVER, NORTH OF MOUNT ST. HELENS. SCIENTISTS HAD WARNED THAT THE VOLCANO COULD ERUPT AT ANY MINUTE, BUT THE FRIENDS WERE NOT WORRIED. THE CAMPSITE WAS WELL OUTSIDE THE DANGER ZONE.

I DON'T KNOW WHY YOU BROUGHT THAT HOUND WITH YOU, TERRY.

TERRY CRALL HAD WOKEN EARLY THAT MORNING TO FISH WHILE HIS GIRLFRIEND, KAREN VARNER, SLEPT. BRUCE NELSON AND SUE RUFF WERE ALSO AWAKE.

ALL SHE'LL DO IS SCARE OFF THE FISH.

SHE'S ENJOYING HERSELF. BESIDES, I NEVER CATCH MUCH ANYWAY.

HEY, BRUCE! BREAKFAST IS ALMOST READY!

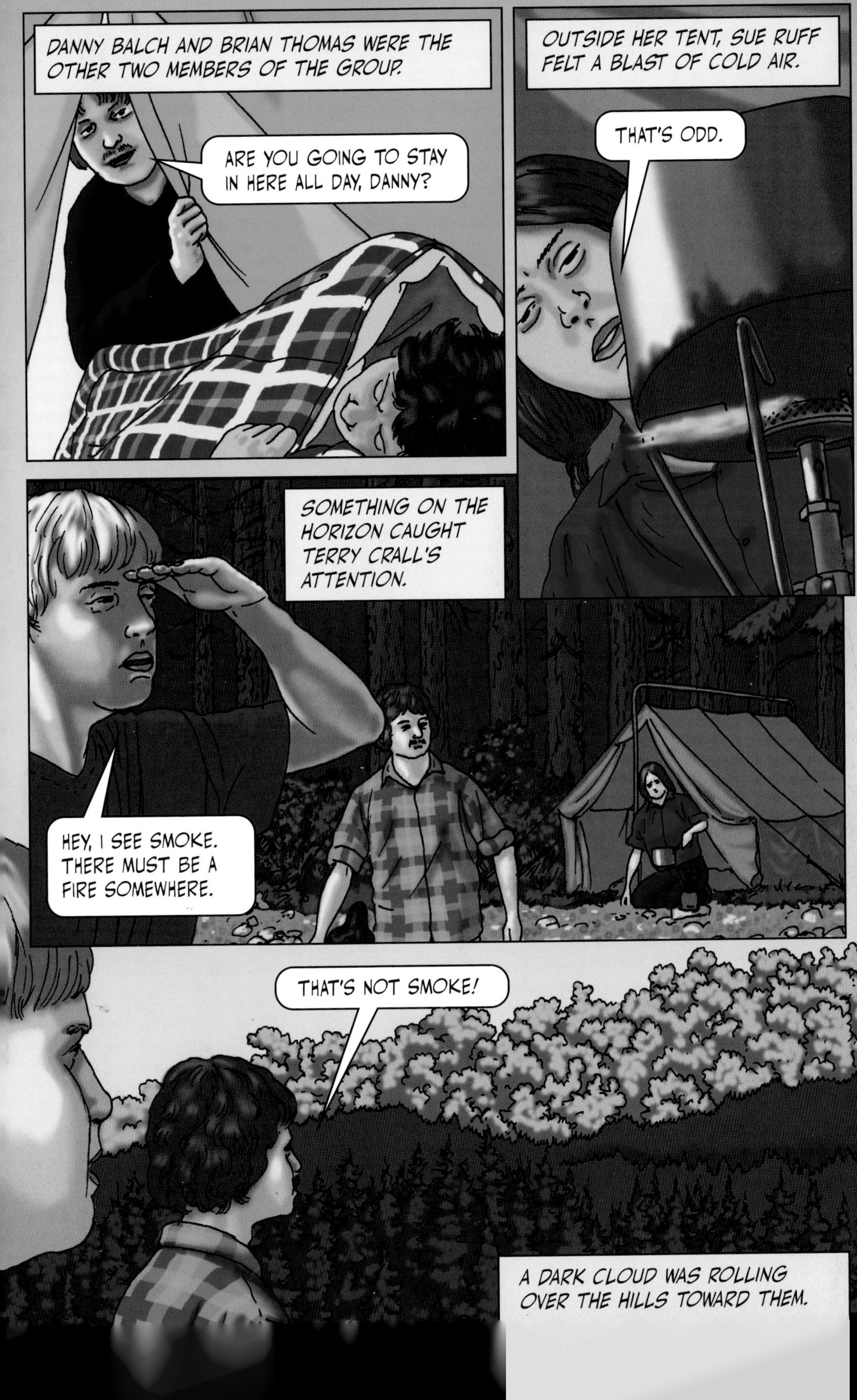
DANNY BALCH AND BRIAN THOMAS WERE THE OTHER TWO MEMBERS OF THE GROUP.
ARE YOU GOING TO STAY IN HERE ALL DAY, DANNY?
OUTSIDE HER TENT, SUE RUFF FELT A BLAST OF COLD AIR.
THAT'S ODD.
SOMETHING ON THE HORIZON CAUGHT TERRY CRALL'S ATTENTION.
HEY, I SEE SMOKE. THERE MUST BE A FIRE SOMEWHERE.
THAT'S NOT SMOKE!
A DARK CLOUD WAS ROLLING OVER THE HILLS TOWARD THEM.

JUST A FEW MINUTES EARLIER MOUNT ST. HELENS HAD PRESENTED A PICTURE OF PEACE AND CALM, ITS SNOW-CAPPED PEAK REFLECTED IN SPIRIT LAKE.

AT 8:32 A.M. AN EARTHQUAKE TRIGGERED AN ERUPTION. THE TOP OF THE MOUNTAIN EXPLODED, CREATING A SUPERHOT CLOUD OF ROCK, ASH, AND STEAM.

BAADDOOMM!

TERRY CRALL RAN TO HIS TENT.
BRUCE NELSON GRABBED SUE RUFF,
AND BRIAN THOMAS THREW HIMSELF
UNDER AN OLD FALLEN TREE.

BRUCE NELSON AND SUE RUFF JUMPED
INTO THE HOLLOW LEFT BY A TREE STUMP.

RUN!

DANNY BALCH HAD LEFT HIS TENT JUST IN TIME TO BE SENT FLYING BY THE ERUPTION'S BLAST WAVE.

HE WAS STILL ON THE GROUND WHEN ICE-COLD MUDDY RAIN BEGAN TO FALL...

...FOLLOWED BY A BOILING CLOUD OF HOT ASH THAT BURNED HIS HANDS, ARMS, AND LEGS.

AFTER A FEW MINUTES THE ROARING STOPPED. DANNY BALCH GOT UP. ALL AROUND HIM WERE BROKEN AND TOPPLED TREES. THE AIR WAS FULL OF ASH.

AT 8:35 A.M. ROALD REITAN CRAWLED OUT OF HIS TENT. HE AND HIS GIRLFRIEND, VENUS DERGAN, WERE CAMPED AT JERICHO HOLE ON THE SOUTH FORK OF THE TOUTLE RIVER.

THEY WERE 30 MILES (48 KM) FROM THE VOLCANO AND DID NOT KNOW THAT IT HAD ERUPTED. AS REITAN WATCHED THE RIVER, HE NOTICED THAT SOMETHING WAS STRANGE ABOUT IT.

STICKS?

THE CLEAR WATER WAS BECOMING CLOUDY, AND TREE BRANCHES WERE FLOATING BY.

THE RIVER'S RISING! AND SO FAST!

THE ERUPTION HAD MELTED ICE AND SNOW FROM THE MOUNTAINSIDE. THE FAST-MOVING MELTWATER, MIXED WITH ASH AND DEBRIS, FORMED AN UNSTOPPABLE MUD SLURRY, CALLED A LAHAR.

IT HAD TAKEN LESS THAN TEN MINUTES FOR THE LAHAR TO REACH JERICHO HOLE. REITAN DASHED BACK TO THE TENT.

ROALD, WHAT IS IT? WHAT'S GOING ON?

VENUS! COME ON! WE HAVE TO GET OUT OF HERE!

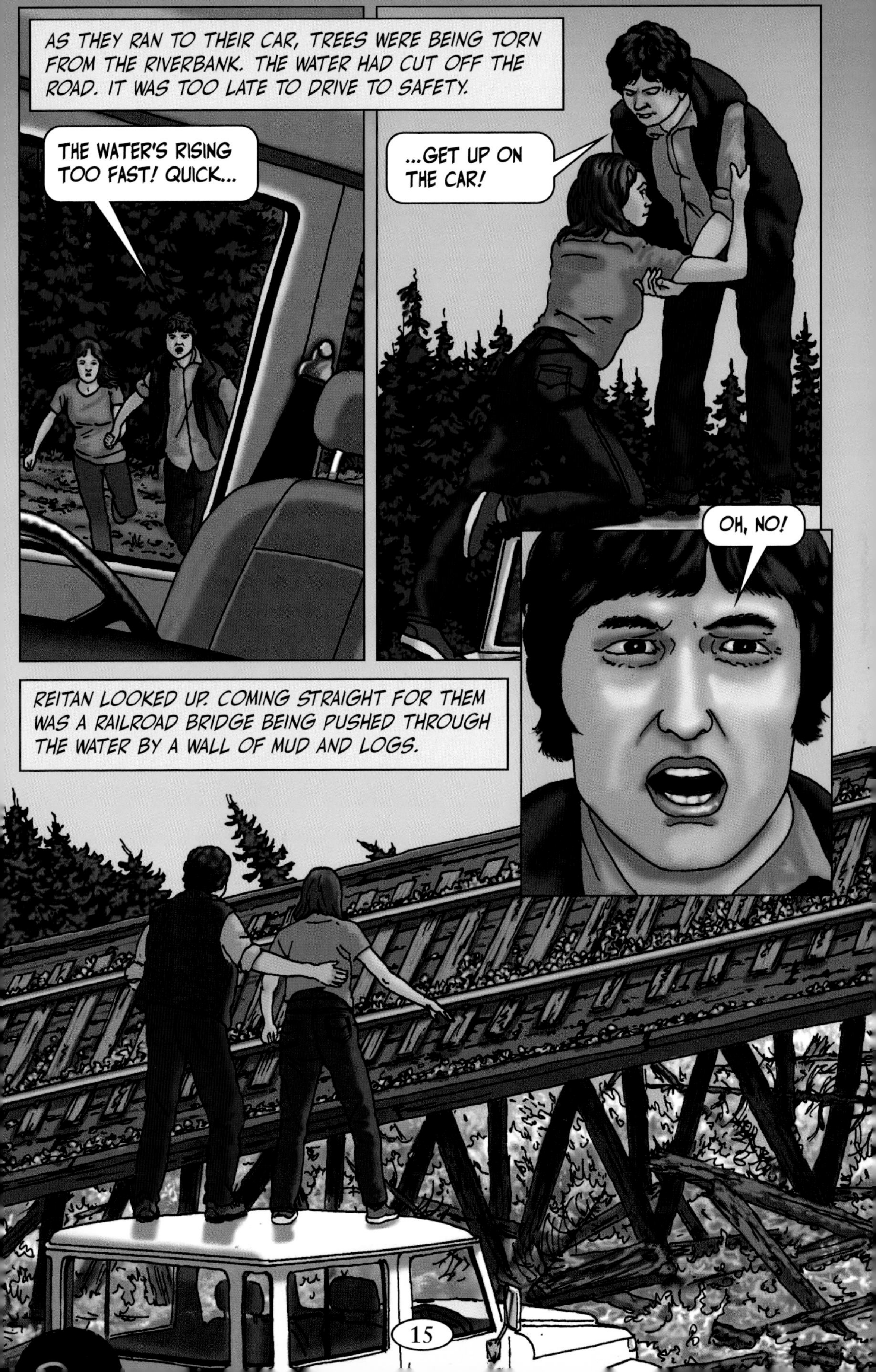
AS THEY RAN TO THEIR CAR, TREES WERE BEING TORN FROM THE RIVERBANK. THE WATER HAD CUT OFF THE ROAD. IT WAS TOO LATE TO DRIVE TO SAFETY.
THE WATER'S RISING TOO FAST! QUICK...
...GET UP ON THE CAR!
OH, NO!
REITAN LOOKED UP. COMING STRAIGHT FOR THEM WAS A RAILROAD BRIDGE BEING PUSHED THROUGH THE WATER BY A WALL OF MUD AND LOGS.

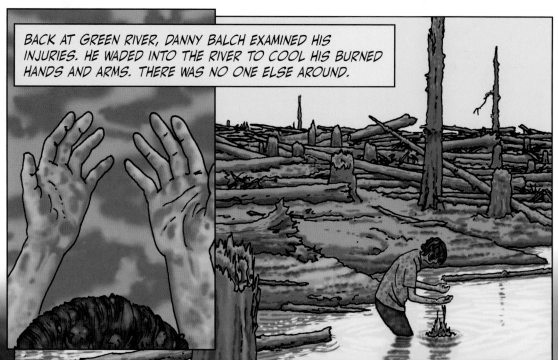

BACK AT GREEN RIVER, DANNY BALCH EXAMINED HIS INJURIES. HE WADED INTO THE RIVER TO COOL HIS BURNED HANDS AND ARMS. THERE WAS NO ONE ELSE AROUND.

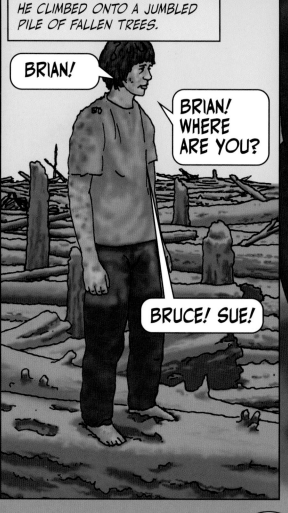

HE CLIMBED ONTO A JUMBLED PILE OF FALLEN TREES.

BRIAN!

BRIAN! WHERE ARE YOU?

BRUCE! SUE!

SUDDENLY...

DANNY! HELP ME!

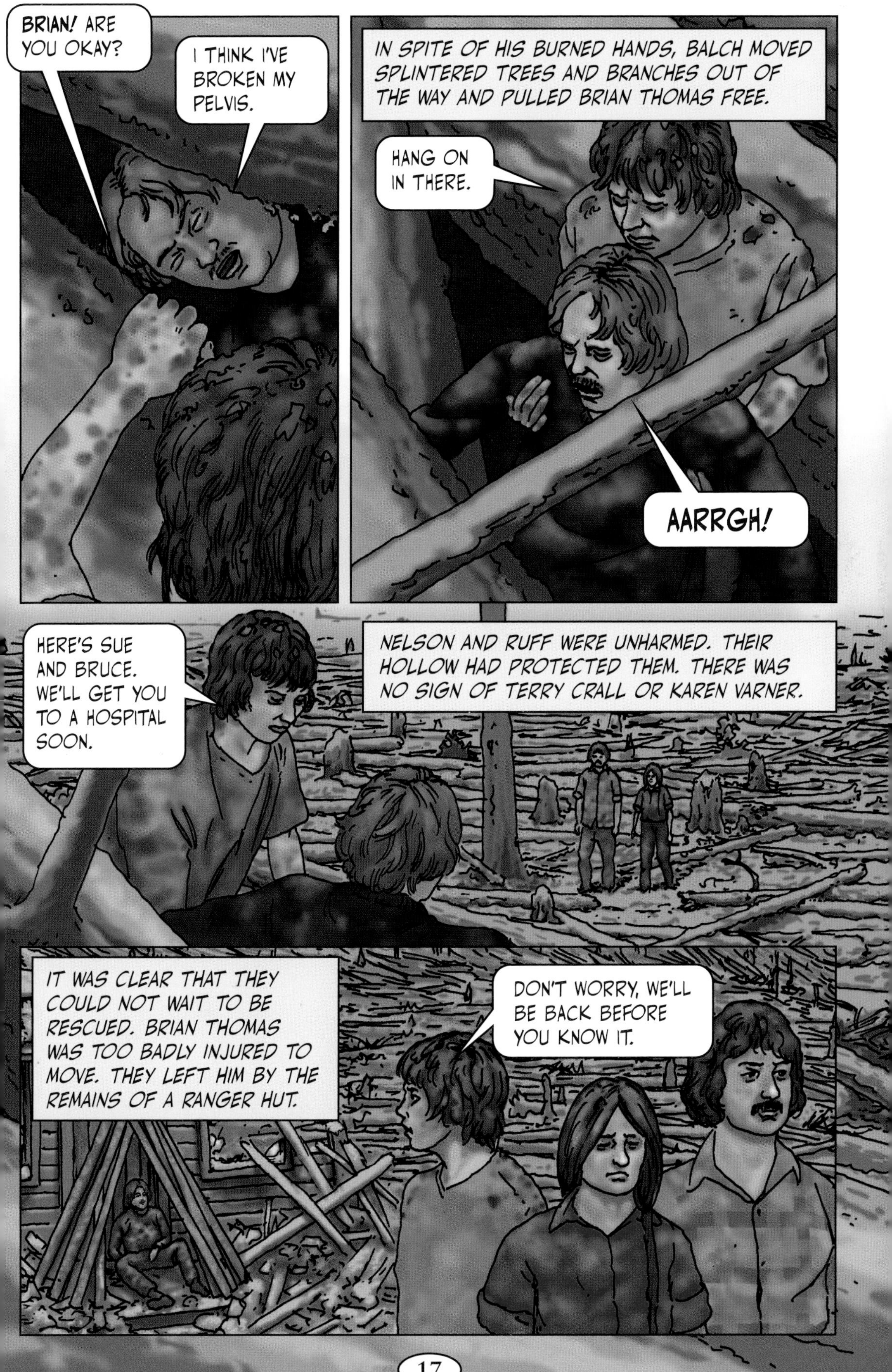
BRIAN! ARE YOU OKAY?
I THINK I'VE BROKEN MY PELVIS.
IN SPITE OF HIS BURNED HANDS, BALCH MOVED SPLINTERED TREES AND BRANCHES OUT OF THE WAY AND PULLED BRIAN THOMAS FREE.
HANG ON IN THERE.
AARRGH!
HERE'S SUE AND BRUCE. WE'LL GET YOU TO A HOSPITAL SOON.
NELSON AND RUFF WERE UNHARMED. THEIR HOLLOW HAD PROTECTED THEM. THERE WAS NO SIGN OF TERRY CRALL OR KAREN VARNER.
IT WAS CLEAR THAT THEY COULD NOT WAIT TO BE RESCUED. BRIAN THOMAS WAS TOO BADLY INJURED TO MOVE. THEY LEFT HIM BY THE REMAINS OF A RANGER HUT.
DON'T WORRY, WE'LL BE BACK BEFORE YOU KNOW IT.

ON THE FLOODED TOUTLE RIVER THE TRESTLE BRIDGE WAS ABOUT TO SMASH INTO THE STRANDED CAR WHEN IT BROKE APART.

THE RIVER IS RISING FAST. WE WON'T BE SAFE HERE FOR LONG.

A RAFT OF TREES FLOATED BY. REITAN SAW A CHANCE TO ESCAPE.

JUMP!

AS HE LANDED, REITAN SLIPPED. HIS KNEE BECAME CAUGHT BETWEEN TWO LOGS.

AAHHH!

HE MANAGED TO CLIMB ONTO THE LOGS. HE COULD NOT SEE HIS GIRLFRIEND AT FIRST. THEN...

VENUS!

...A HAND ROSE ABOVE THE WATER. REITAN GRABBED IT...

...BUT IT SLIPPED.

VENUS DERGAN DISAPPEARED BENEATH THE WATER OF THE FLOODED RIVER.

VENUS! NO!

ON THE GREEN RIVER, DANNY BALCH WAS HAVING PROBLEMS. HE HAD LEFT HIS TENT WITHOUT HIS SHOES, AND THE HOT ASH WAS BURNING HIS BARE FEET.

IT'S NO USE. I CAN'T GO ON.

OKAY, DANNY, YOU STAY HERE, CLOSE TO THE RIVER. WE'LL SEND HELP JUST AS SOON AS WE CAN.

BRUCE NELSON AND SUE RUFF KEPT HEADING NORTH OUT OF THE DISASTER ZONE.

ON THE TOUTLE RIVER, ROALD REITAN PLUNGED HIS HAND INTO THE MUDDY WATER.

HE FELT HAIR, GRABBED HOLD OF IT, AND HEAVED. UP CAME VENUS DERGAN.

GASP!

REITAN PULLED HER ONTO THE LOGS. SHE WAS CUT AND BRUISED BUT NOT BADLY HURT. EVENTUALLY, THE LOG RAFT DRIFTED INTO SHALLOW WATER AND THEY WADED ASHORE.

THEY CLIMBED TO HIGHER GROUND. THE RAFT HAD CARRIED THEM 3 MILES (4.8 KM) FROM WHERE THEY HAD CAMPED.

AT THE GREEN RIVER CAMPSITE, BRIAN THOMAS WAS BEGINNING TO GET COLD. DANNY BALCH'S CAR WAS PARKED AT THE TOP OF THE TRAIL. IF HE COULD REACH IT, HE COULD GET WARM AGAIN. HE STARTED TO CRAWL.

AAGHH!

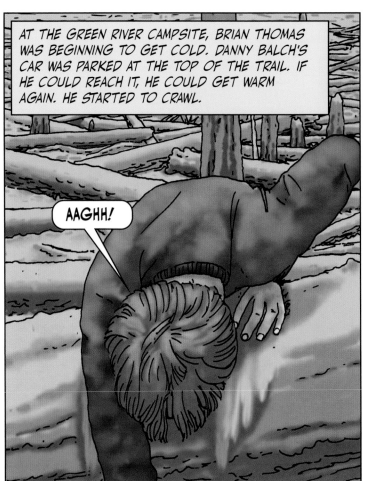

HE HAD GONE LESS THAN 100 YARDS (91.4 M) WHEN HE HEARD A NOISE.

A HELICOPTER WAS HOVERING ABOVE HIM. HE WAS SAVED.

NELSON AND RUFF HAD BEEN PICKED UP EARLIER AND HAD TOLD THE HELICOPTER PILOT WHERE TO FIND THOMAS AND BALCH.

A HELICOPTER HAD ALSO SPOTTED ROALD REITAN AND VENUS DERGAN. THEY WERE SOON AIRLIFTED TO SAFETY.

THOCK THOCK

ED "BUZZ" SMITH AND HIS TWO SONS HAD FOUND DANNY BALCH. SMITH HAD A SPARE PAIR OF SHOES THAT HE GAVE TO BALCH. TOGETHER, THEY HIKED 9 MILES (14.5 KM) TO A CLEARING, WHERE THEY WERE RESCUED BY A HELICOPTER.

THE HELICOPTER PILOTS OF THE AIR NATIONAL GUARD WERE BUSY OVER THE NEXT FEW DAYS, LOOKING FOR SURVIVORS AND VICTIMS.

THE SCALE OF DEVASTATION CAUSED BY THE ERUPTION WAS IMMENSE. EVERY TREE IN A 230-SQUARE-MILE (595.5-SQ-KM) AREA HAD BEEN BLOWN DOWN AND CARPETED WITH GRAY ASH.

ON MAY 23, BRUCE NELSON WENT BACK TO THE CAMPSITE TO LOOK FOR HIS FRIENDS TERRY CRALL AND KAREN VARNER. HE FOUND THEIR BODIES STILL IN THEIR TENT. THEY HAD BEEN CRUSHED BY A FALLING TREE. THEIR PET DOG WAS BROUGHT OUT ALIVE.

IT'S OKAY, GIRL. YOU'RE SAFE NOW.

IN THE FOLLOWING DAYS AND WEEKS OTHER SURVIVAL TALES EMERGED. MIKE AND LU MOORE AND THEIR TWO DAUGHTERS ESCAPED THE VOLCANO'S BLAST AND DEADLY ASH CLOUD BY HIDING IN A RUNDOWN HUNTER'S SHACK.

LOGGER JAMES SCYMANKY AND THREE COWORKERS WERE CAUGHT IN THE BLAST. ALL FOUR WERE BADLY BURNED BUT STILL TRIED TO WALK OUT OF THE DISASTER AREA. ONLY SCYMANKY SURVIVED.

THE GLOWING CLOUD OF RED-HOT ASH CHASED CHARLES MCNERNEY AND JOHN SMART IN THEIR CAR FOR OVER 5 MILES (8 KM) BEFORE THEY FINALLY MANAGED TO OUTRUN IT.

A FEW WEEKS AFTER THE ERUPTION THE FIRST GREEN SHOOTS OF LIFE APPEARED IN THE GRAY LANDSCAPE. ANIMAL TRACKS COULD BE FOUND BETWEEN THE YOUNG PLANTS. IN SPITE OF THE TERRIBLE DAMAGE THE VOLCANO HAD CAUSED, THE BIGGEST SURVIVOR HAD BEEN NATURE ITSELF.

THE END

ALONE AND INJURED IN THE AFRICAN BUSH

HWANGE NATIONAL PARK, ZIMBABWE, 2003

IT IS 9:15 A.M. AND GREG RASMUSSEN IS FLYING HIGH ABOVE THE ROUGH TERRAIN OF THE AFRICAN BUSH IN A SINGLE-ENGINED ULTRALIGHT. HE HAS JUST PICKED UP THE SIGNAL FROM THE RADIO COLLAR OF A LOST RHINO HE HAS BEEN SEARCHING FOR.

THE AIR IS HOT AND THIN, WHICH MAKES FLYING DIFFICULT. AS HE TURNS INTO A DIVE TO TAKE A CLOSER LOOK, HE LOSES CONTROL OF HIS PLANE.

THERE IS NOTHING HE CAN DO TO REGAIN CONTROL AS THE PLANE SPINS TO EARTH AT 120 MPH (193 KPH).

I'M GOING TO CRASH!

THE PLANE HITS THE GROUND WITH A SICKENING CRUNCH.

26

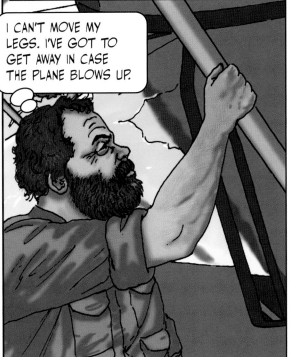

GREG WAKES UP IN THE COCKPIT. FUEL IS LEAKING ALL OVER HIM. HE CRAWLS AWAY FROM THE WRECKAGE AS QUICKLY AS HE CAN.

I CAN'T MOVE MY LEGS. I'VE GOT TO GET AWAY IN CASE THE PLANE BLOWS UP.

I FORGOT TO MAKE A MAYDAY CALL. I'M GOING TO HAVE TO GO BACK.

MAYDAY, MAYDAY...

THE RADIO IS BROKEN BEYOND REPAIR.

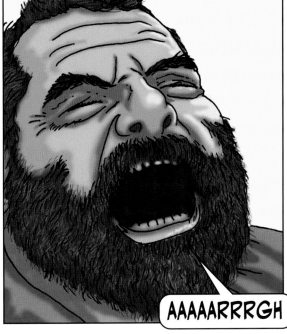

GREG HAS BROKEN MOST OF THE BONES IN HIS LEGS AND FEET. AS THE SHOCK FROM THE CRASH WEARS OFF HE BEGINS TO FEEL THE PAIN.

AAAAARRRGH

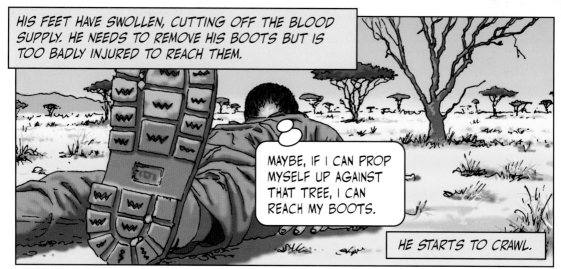

HIS FEET HAVE SWOLLEN, CUTTING OFF THE BLOOD SUPPLY. HE NEEDS TO REMOVE HIS BOOTS BUT IS TOO BADLY INJURED TO REACH THEM.

MAYBE, IF I CAN PROP MYSELF UP AGAINST THAT TREE, I CAN REACH MY BOOTS.

HE STARTS TO CRAWL.

LATER.

OW! JUST MY LUCK, IT'S A THORN TREE.

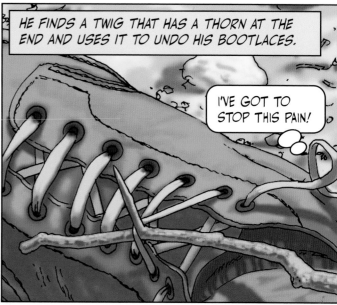

HE FINDS A TWIG THAT HAS A THORN AT THE END AND USES IT TO UNDO HIS BOOTLACES.

I'VE GOT TO STOP THIS PAIN!

THIS IS GOING TO HURT.

AFTER TWO-AND-A-HALF HOURS HE MANAGES TO UNLACE BOTH BOOTS. THERE IS NO RELIEF, HIS FEET HAVE SWOLLEN INSIDE THEM. HE GRABS A NEARBY STICK TO PUSH THE BOOTS OFF. HE PUTS ANOTHER STICK IN HIS MOUTH TO BITE ON AGAINST THE PAIN.

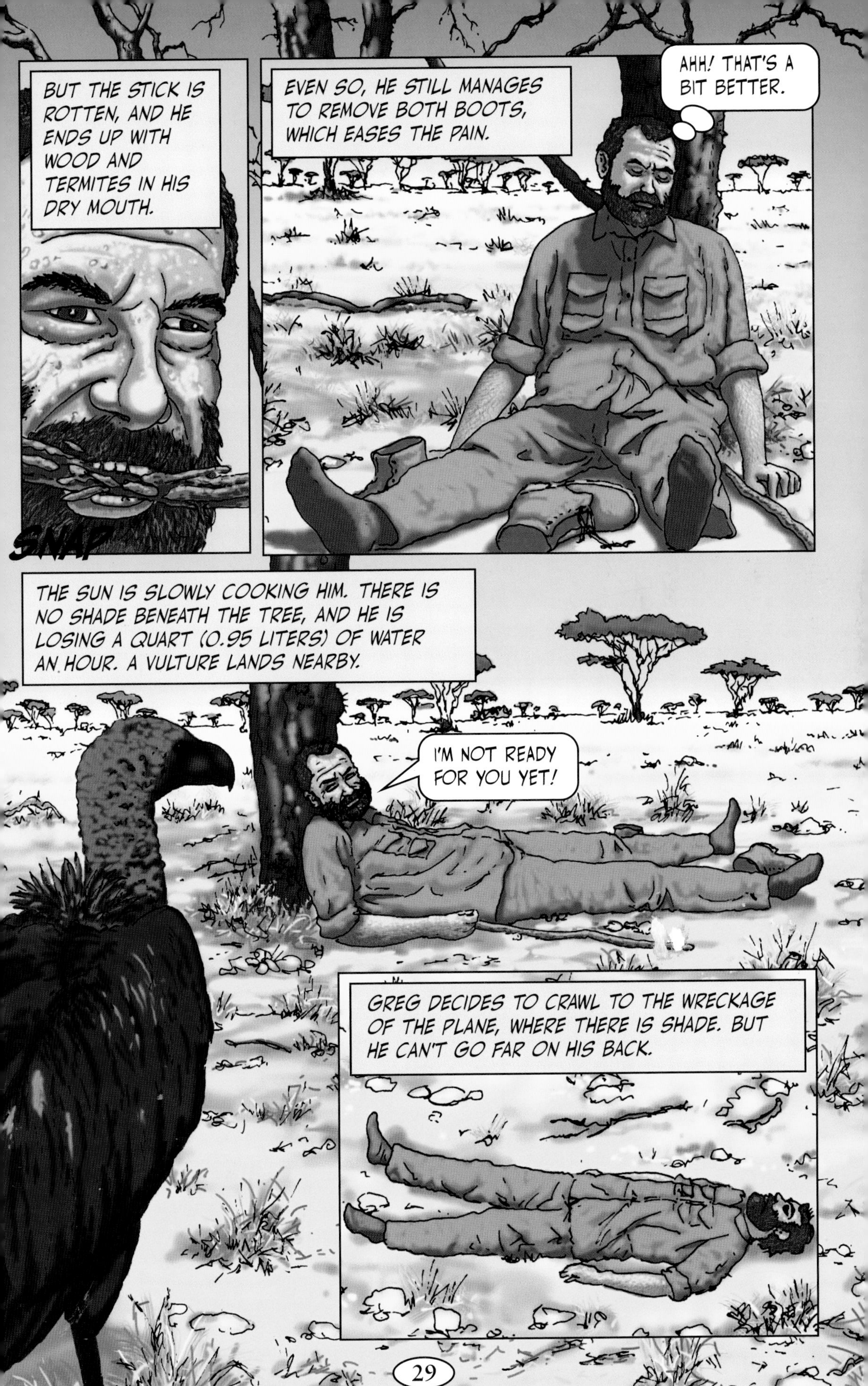
BUT THE STICK IS ROTTEN, AND HE ENDS UP WITH WOOD AND TERMITES IN HIS DRY MOUTH.
SNAP
EVEN SO, HE STILL MANAGES TO REMOVE BOTH BOOTS, WHICH EASES THE PAIN.
AHH! THAT'S A BIT BETTER.
THE SUN IS SLOWLY COOKING HIM. THERE IS NO SHADE BENEATH THE TREE, AND HE IS LOSING A QUART (0.95 LITERS) OF WATER AN HOUR. A VULTURE LANDS NEARBY.
I'M NOT READY FOR YOU YET!
GREG DECIDES TO CRAWL TO THE WRECKAGE OF THE PLANE, WHERE THERE IS SHADE. BUT HE CAN'T GO FAR ON HIS BACK.

REPTILES CRAWL LOW TO THE GROUND. I'LL USE LESS ENERGY IF I DO IT ON MY FRONT.

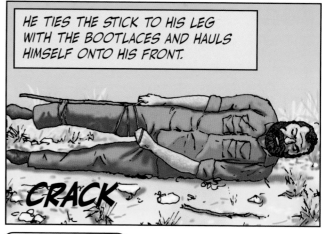

HE TIES THE STICK TO HIS LEG WITH THE BOOTLACES AND HAULS HIMSELF ONTO HIS FRONT.

CRACK

AAAARRRRGH

GREG DISCOVERS HE ALSO HAS A BROKEN PELVIS.

DESPITE THE PAIN, HE MANAGES TO CRAWL FORWARD, BUT STOPS SUDDENLY WHEN HE HEARS A FAMILIAR NOISE.

OH, NO!

IT IS THE DISTINCTIVE SOUND OF ELEPHANTS, AND THEY ARE HEADING HIS WAY. IF THEY GET TOO CLOSE BEFORE THEY SEE HIM, HE MIGHT BE TRAMPLED TO DEATH.

PLEASE DON'T TRAMPLE ME!

LUCKILY, THE ELEPHANTS SENSE THAT SOMETHING IS WRONG AND TURN AWAY.

BY 4:00 P.M. GREG IS IN THE SHADE OF THE PLANE WRECKAGE.

BUT THINGS GO FROM BAD TO WORSE. HE HEARS THE SOUND OF A LION. A FEMALE AND HER CUBS ARE COMING TOWARD HIM.

THE LIONESS GETS CLOSER.

ANIMALS THREATENED BY PREDATORS OFTEN SCARE THEM OFF BY MAKING A LOUD NOISE.

31

HE STRIKES THE PLANE'S SIDES WITH A STICK.

BANG
BANG
BANG

THE LIONESS LEAPS AWAY.

IT WORKED!

AT 5:00 P.M. HE HEARS A PLANE. IT IS ONE OF THE SEARCH TEAMS, BUT IT DOES NOT SEE HIM.

I MUST STAY ALIVE.

DARKNESS FALLS, AND WITH IT COMES THE TERROR OF THE NIGHT ANIMALS.

AT 1.00 A.M...

WHAT'S THAT SOUND?

HYENA!

GREG TRIES THE SAME TACTIC HE USED AGAINST THE LIONESS...

...AND IT WORKS.

AT 10:30 A.M. HE IS SEEN BY A PARK RANGER IN A SPOTTER PLANE. A SHORT TIME LATER, FRIENDS AND RESCUERS ARRIVE. GREG HAS SURVIVED AGAINST ALL THE ODDS.

THE END

33

LOST IN THE SNOW
ANSEL ADAMS WILDERNESS,
SIERRA NEVADA, CALIFORNIA, 2004

ON FEBRUARY 6, ERIC LEMARQUE IS SITTING ON DRAGON'S BACK RIDGE AT MAMMOTH MOUNTAIN SKI RESORT. IT IS GETTING COLD AS THE SUN HOVERS JUST ABOVE THE MOUNTAIN.

I HOPE THE JACUZZI'S WARM, BECAUSE IN TEN MINUTES THAT'S WHERE I'M GOING TO BE.

TWO SKI PATROLLERS START THEIR DAILY RITUAL OF SHUTTING DOWN THE RUNS.

ONE OF THE PATROLLERS SKIS OVER TO ERIC. THEY NOD AT EACH OTHER.

TIME TO GO FOR MY LAST RUN.

ERIC STRAPS ON HIS SNOWBOARD.

BRRR. I SHOULD WARM UP WHEN I GET GOING.

HE IS ONLY WEARING A JACKET AND SKI PANTS WITH NO LINING, A T-SHIRT, A PAIR OF LONG JOHNS, A PAIR OF SOCKS AND GLOVES, AND TWO SKI HATS.

ERIC LAUNCHES HIMSELF DOWN THE OUT-OF-BOUNDS RUN.

THE SNOW IS SMOOTH AND UNTOUCHED.

JUST GO WITH THE FLOW.

THE CLOUDS FORM QUICKLY, AND ERIC SUDDENLY FINDS HIMSELF IN A THICK FOG.

I CAN BARELY SEE A THING.

ERIC REMOVES HIS GOGGLES TO SEE BETTER. THE WIND BLINDS HIM.

WHERE AM I?

THE RUN FLATTENS OUT, AND HE SINKS INTO THE SOFT SNOW.

ISN'T THIS RUN SUPPOSED TO LEAD ME OUT?

ERIC UNCLIPS HIS BOARD AND STARTS TO WALK.

THIS IS NOT GOOD. THERE HAS TO BE A WAY OUT OF HERE.

HE WALKS WEST TOWARD THE MOUNTAIN. IT IS GETTING DARKER AND COLDER. SOMETIMES THE SNOW COMES UP TO HIS CHEST.

AM I LOST?

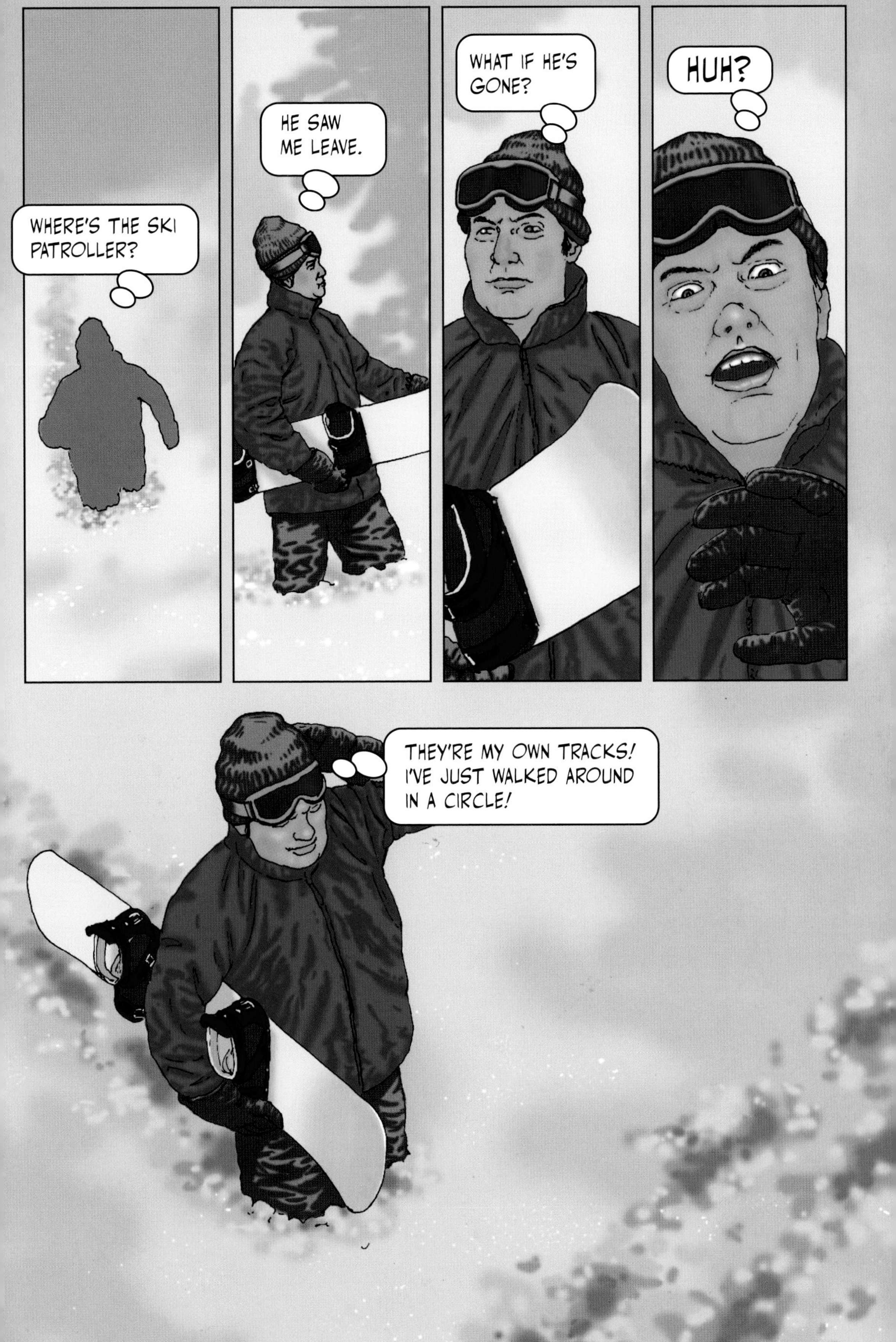
WHERE'S THE SKI PATROLLER?
HE SAW ME LEAVE.
WHAT IF HE'S GONE?
HUH?
THEY'RE MY OWN TRACKS! I'VE JUST WALKED AROUND IN A CIRCLE!

OKAY, I'LL GO BACK UP THE MOUNTAIN AND TRY TO RETRACE MY STEPS. I'LL FIND A SKI RUN AND FOLLOW THAT.

AS IT GETS DARK, ERIC DECIDES TO STOP FOR THE NIGHT. HE TRIES TO KEEP WARM BY BURNING SOME OF HIS CLOTHES.

THE MATCHES WON'T LIGHT. THEY'VE GOTTEN WET.

USING HIS SNOWBOARD, HE SCRAPES BARK OFF A TREE AND BREAKS OFF SOME BRANCHES...

THIS WIND IS CUTTING RIGHT THROUGH ME.

...WHICH HE PUTS INTO A HOLLOW HE HAS SCRAPED OUT OF THE SNOW.

AT LEAST I WON'T BE LYING ON THE COLD SNOW.

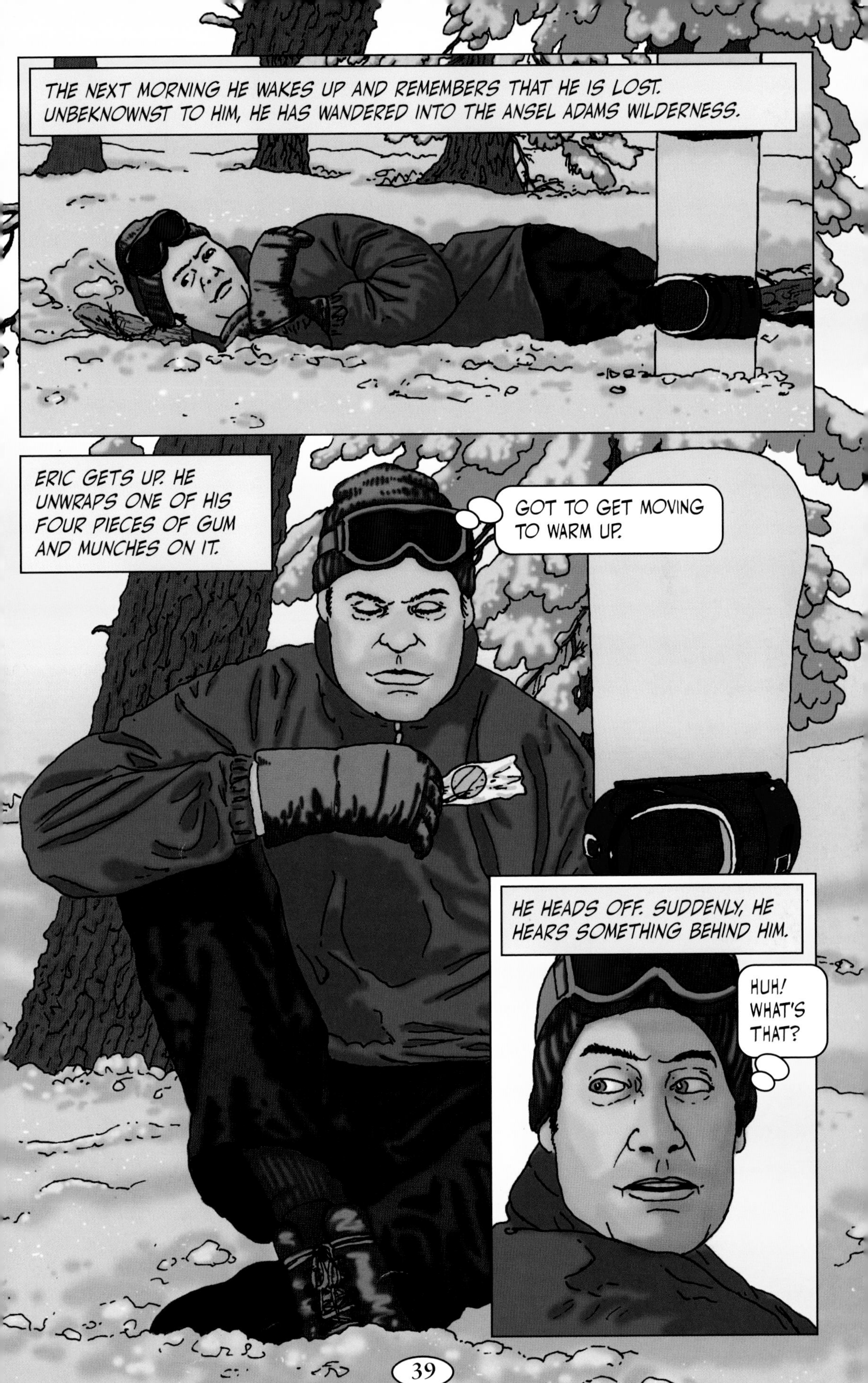
THE NEXT MORNING HE WAKES UP AND REMEMBERS THAT HE IS LOST. UNBEKNOWNST TO HIM, HE HAS WANDERED INTO THE ANSEL ADAMS WILDERNESS.
ERIC GETS UP. HE UNWRAPS ONE OF HIS FOUR PIECES OF GUM AND MUNCHES ON IT.
GOT TO GET MOVING TO WARM UP.
HE HEADS OFF. SUDDENLY, HE HEARS SOMETHING BEHIND HIM.
HUH! WHAT'S THAT?

NOT FAR AWAY ARE TWO COYOTES.

MAYBE THEY CAN SMELL MY GUM.

ERIC SWALLOWS THE GUM HE IS CHEWING AND THROWS AWAY THE OTHER PIECES.

LUCKILY, HE NEVER SEES THEM AGAIN. WHEN HE IS HUNGRY HE EATS BARK AND PINE NUTS.

MMMM. NOT BAD.

OCCASIONALLY HE SNOWBOARDS DOWN SLOPES TO SAVE ENERGY.

ON THE FOURTH DAY, HIS CLOTHES ARE SO WET HE TAKES THEM ALL OFF AND LAYS THEM OUT TO DRY. HE WEDGES HIMSELF IN A CRACK IN THE ROCKS TO KEEP OUT OF THE COLD WIND.

OUCH! MY FEET ARE IN A BAD WAY.

WHEN HE TRIES TO PUT HIS BOOTS BACK ON, HIS FEET ARE TOO SWOLLEN. HE MANAGES TO GET ONE BOOT ON WITHOUT A SOCK.

THAT'LL HAVE TO DO. I'VE GOT TO KEEP MOVING TO STAY WARM.

WHILE LISTENING TO A RADIO STATION ON HIS MP3 PLAYER, HE MAKES A STUNNING DISCOVERY. HE CAN WORK OUT THE DIRECTION OF THE STATION (AND CIVILIZATION)...

...AND HEADS OFF IN THE DIRECTION OF THE STRONGEST SIGNAL.

ERIC CLIMBS 1,200 FEET (365 M) UP A STEEP SLOPE. HIS FEET ARE GETTING WORSE AND HE IS BECOMING DELIRIOUS.

I NEED TO GET HOME.

WHUP
WHUP
WHUP

I GIVE UP... WAIT. WHAT'S THAT NOISE?

WHUP
WHUP
WHUP

SKI PATROLLERS HAD PICKED UP ERIC'S SNOWBOARD TRAIL ON FEBRUARY 13, AND ALERTED HELICOPTER SEARCH TEAMS. ERIC WAS RESCUED FROM PUMICE BUTTE AND TAKEN TO THE HOSPITAL, WHERE IT WAS DISCOVERED THAT HIS FEET WERE FROZEN AND HAD TO BE AMPUTATED. SINCE THEN, ERIC LEMARQUE HAS MADE AN AMAZING RECOVERY AND IS SNOWBOARDING AGAIN WITH PROSTHETIC LOWER LEGS.

THE END

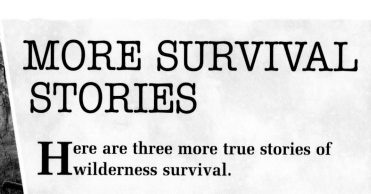

MORE SURVIVAL STORIES

Here are three more true stories of wilderness survival.

LEFT FOR DEAD

It was August 1822, on the Grand River, South Dakota. Frontiersman Hugh Glass was a member of an expedition trekking up the Missouri River. He was alone, hunting for game, when he surprised a grizzly bear. It attacked Glass, biting and ripping him with its claws. Luckily, two of Glass's expedition partners were nearby and killed the animal.

Glass's injuries were severe. The expedition leader thought he would not live through the night. Two men were left behind to bury Glass when he died, while the rest moved on. After three days, Glass was unconscious but still alive. The two men became tired of waiting and left, taking Glass's gun and knife. Glass awoke alone, wrapped in the skin of the bear that had attacked him. His wounds were infected, and his leg was broken.

The nearest settlement, Fort Kiowa, was 200 miles (322 km) away. He began to crawl. When he was young, Glass had been taught by Pawnee tribesmen how to live off the land. He put that knowledge to use as he dragged himself through the bush searching for roots and wild berries. After two months, Glass reached the Cheyenne River. He built a raft and drifted downstream to the Missouri River. Four months later he limped into Fort Kiowa.

STROKE OF LUCK

It was 2005, and experienced backpacker Amy Racina was 12 days into her hike through Kings Canyon National Park, California. She had lost the trail and was trying to to find it again when she slipped, and fell 60 feet (18.2 m) onto rocks.

Amy tried to move but could not. Her legs and left hip were shattered, but she was lucky to be alive after such a fall. Fortunately her backpack was next to her, and she was able to tend her injuries, keep warm, eat, and drink. She was in a remote area, though, and the chances of being found by another hiker were slim. But on the fourth day her desperate cries for help were heard by Jake Van Akkeren–incredibly, a man who suffered from hearing loss— and she was airlifted to a hospital. Luck played a big part in Amy Racina's rescue and survival.

OUTBACK HORROR

Ricky Megee's ordeal began in January 2006. He had been driving to Port Headland in northern Australia when he stopped to pick up a stranger. The next thing he remembered was waking up face down in a ditch in the middle of nowhere. His shoes, money, and SUV were gone, and he had no idea how he had gotten there.

For the next ten days Megee wandered through the scrub with temperatures reaching 105°F (40°C). He found a natural dam and spent the 60 days camped by its side. He survived by eating insects, lizards, and frogs. The bugs didn't taste good, but the leeches were not too bad, he later claimed. Most things he ate raw (although the frogs he skewered on sticks and sun-dried until they were crisp). After 71 days he was rescued, 132 lbs (59 kg) lighter, and still unsure how he gotten lost in the first place.

GLOSSARY

coniferous Mostly evergreen trees that have needle or scale-like leaves and cones.

coyotes A wild dog that is similar to a wolf.

deciduous Shedding leaves seasonally.

delirious Having a confused and agitated state of mind.

devastation Severe destruction.

distinctive A unique characteristic.

fens Low-lying marshy areas.

frontiersman A person who lives and works in a wilderness.

fungi The group of living organisms that includes mushrooms and toadstools.

immense Very large.

Jacuzzi A large bath that massages the occupants by means of underwater jets.

larva The early form of an insect before it changes into an adult.

leeches A type of blood-sucking worm.

Mayday The international distress signal used by ships and aircraft.

meltwater Streams or rivers formed from melted snow and ice.

odds The chances of something happening.

pelvis The large bone at the center of the body, to which the backbone and legs are attached.

predators An animal that hunts others for food.

prosthetic An artificial part of the body.

remains A part of something that is left over.

retrace To go back over one's steps.

skewered Food that has been pierced through with a stick or metal rod.

slurry Watery mud.

SUV Short for sport-utility vehicle.

tactic A plan to achieve a goal.

terrain An area of land and its physical features.

tracts Large areas of land.

trampled Being crushed underfoot.

threatened Intended harm.

FOR MORE INFORMATION

ORGANIZATIONS

American Wilderness Coalition
122 C Street, NW
Suite 240
Washington, DC 10001-2109
(202) 266 0455
Web site: http://www.americanwilderness.org

US Forest Service
1400 Independence Ave, SW
Washington, DC 20250-0003
(800) 832 1355
Web site: http://www.fs.fed.us

FURTHER READING

Lewis, Brenda Ralph. *Wilderness Rescue with the United States Search and Rescue Task Force*. Broomall, PA: Mason Crest Publishers, 2003.

Llewellyn, Claire. *Survive In the Jungle* (Survival Challenge). London, England: Andromeda Children's Books, 2006.

McNab, Chris. *The Boy's Book of Outdoor Survival: 101 Courageous Skills for Exploring the Dangerous Wild*. Berkeley, CA: Ulysses Press, 2008.

O'Shei, Tim. *Alone in the Wilderness! Brenna Hawkins' Story of Survival*. Bloomington, MN: Capstone Press, 2007.

O'Shei, Tim. *Left for Dead! Lincoln Hall's Story of Survival*. Bloomington, MN: Capstone Press, 2007.

INDEX

Web Sites

Due to the changing nature of Internet links, Rosen Publishing has developed an online list of Web sites related to the subject of this book. This site is updated regularly. Please use this link to access the list:

http://www.rosenlinks.com/ddss/unde